*A girl who was a severe bully magnet
lays down some crooked tracks
and changes the journey of her life...*

THE BUMPS IN THE ROAD
vignettes

Marjorie J. Levine

The Three Tomatoes Book Publishing

Copyright © 2025 by Marjorie J. Levine

All rights reserved. No part of this book may be reproduced in any form or by any electronic or mechanical means, including information storage and retrieval systems, without permission in writing from the publisher. The only exception is by a reviewer, who may quote short excerpts in a review. For permission requests, please address The Three Tomatoes Publishing.

Published: January 2026

Paperback ISBN 979-8-9947313-0-7
Hardcover ISBN 979-8-9947313-1-4
Library of Congress Control Number: 2026902538

For information address:
The Three Tomatoes Book Publishing
6 Soundview Rd.
Glen Cove, NY 11542

Cover photo and interior photo: courtesy of Marjorie J. Levine
Cover and interior design: Susan Herbst

This is a work of nonfiction. Some names and identifying details have been changed to protect the privacy of individuals. The events described are based on the author's recollections and interpretations.

All product names, trademarks, and registered trademarks are property of their respective owners. Mention of these products and trademarks is for informational purposes only and does not imply endorsement or affiliation with the author or publisher.

*For my mother, who gave me nothing,
so I learned how to give myself almost everything.*

Contents

Part One: Real Talk

    All I Have Ever Been and All I Will Never Be 3
    I Used to Live Here as a Kid 9

Part Two: Misery Had No Company

    Joe's Camp 13
    The First Experience at Sleep-Away Summer Camp 15
    Summer Memories with Margaret Bourke-White 17
    My European Vacation 19
    Reflections on Misery and Magical Thinking 23

Part Three: The Face That Could Have Launched 1,000 Hips

    Fantasies, Lies, and Decades Later... the Internet 31
    Al Goldstein and Me 35

Part Four: A Stream Of Consciousness

    Memories of the Stylers 39
    Michael Gazzo Asks Permission 43
    Intermission: Lighten Up! 45

Part Five: My Mosh Pit

    Three Love Letters 49
    The Milgram Experiment and Me 53
    Me and My Baby Teeth 55
    A Ghost Story 57

Part Six: Aliases For Potential Crybabies

    MarjTheBombshell and Solly Boy, the Enforcer 61
    Dumped by Benjamin Weiner 65
    Catfished 69

Part Seven: Always Leave Them Wanting More

    Bessie and the Expensive Coffin Theory 75
    My Mother Makes Joan Crawford
        Look Like Carol Brady 77
    Philosophy from The Crib 79
    A Sunken Corridor 81

Thanks 83
About the Author 85

Part One

Real Talk

2 ~ *The Bumps in the Road: vignettes*

All I Have Ever Been and All I Will Never Be

AT THE EARLY AGE OF FIVE, I had unique talents. I could rattle off the names of all the Brooklyn Dodgers. I could eat a Charlotte Russe in three bites. And at the age of six, when nobody came to pick me up after a day in first grade at Brooklyn's PS 229, I walked all the way home alone. Alone. It was a sign.

In about 1965, I began taking acting classes at HB Studio on Bank Street in Manhattan. I drove there every Sunday from Valley Stream, in my 1962 beige Corvair, with my friend Linda. My teacher was James Patterson, and for one glorious moment in time, my acting partner was Robert DeNiro. We did a scene from the play *The Diary of Anne Frank*. I was just awful. He must have loathed doing the scene with me because after that Sunday, he never returned to class. Time passed.

I finished college at C.W. Post, and I began teaching in Manhattan in 1968. It was probably in the 1970s that I enrolled in nighttime classes at The Lee Strasberg Theater Institute. My instructor was Ernie Martin. We did some improv in his classes, and one night we sat in a circle and some guy next to me passed me an imaginary doobie from which he had just taken a fake hit. He pretended to be high, and I hesitated, trying to decide how to handle that. I looked around at all the other students in that group, all pretending to be stoned, and I pushed his hand away, and I burst into hysterical laughter. I could not stop laughing. I was out of control, exhibiting a Pseudobulbar Affect. I thought my head was going to explode. That evening would become the barometer through the decades by which I would evaluate all other situations to determine if they were humor worthy.

It was in about 1986 when my thoughts turned to becoming serious about show business and becoming a star. I had taken another scene study class in the 1970s at HB Studio with Bill Hickey so I enrolled in a class with him again. I was Blanche in *A Streetcar Named Desire* and that scene received good feedback. I was filled with hope.

In 1987, I enrolled in Weist-Barron and took a few classes in acting for commercials and soap operas. When those sessions ended, I was like a bolt of lightning. I discovered stand-up comedy.

I began a class at The Comic Strip with Rob Weinstein, took a comedy class at The Manhattan Punchline with Gabe Abelson, and then a class at The New School with Scott Blakeman. I was a professional student. I was happy in stand-up. I even won a major contest in 1991 at Stand-up NY Comedy Club to find New York City's funniest teacher. I was on a roll!

I joined AFTRA and had some shitty headshots taken. Trust me, they were horrendous. I never worked in anything where belonging to AFTRA even mattered or was necessary, but I liked being in AFTRA. It made me feel like I was making progress. After many years of paying dues for totally nothing, I asked for an "honorary withdrawal" and received it. That was before AFTRA merged with SAG. If the merger had been in place, I don't think I would have asked for an honorary withdrawal. I was a stickler for details that would fuel my dream of becoming a Hollywood movie star, and being in SAG would have enhanced my delusions. My fantasy world needed layers down a defined rabbit hole.

I had written an episode for the TV sitcom *Seinfeld* and sent it for consideration in representation to a talent agency. ICM must have liked it, because after they received it, instead of tossing it into the circular file, they sent it to the producers of that show, and I received a kind rejection in a reply from Tim Kaiser! I later performed the entire episode on my own broadcast. It broke the internet. I was trending and a viral sensation.

Back to the past. I had taken two sabbaticals from teaching and completed thirty credits above my master's degree. I moved up in the Board of Education pay scale and was moving closer to a point where I could retire. My eye was on the prize at that point: the almighty pension. Finally, the last day on the job arrived. On that day, I waited for the bus that would take me back home and into my new future. One door closed, and I hoped another would open.

Soon thereafter, for fun, I volunteered at The Museum of Television and Radio, now The Paley Center. I loved that little gig: helping visitors in the museum locate on tapes the TV shows from long ago for which they had fond memories. But I was fired from that volunteer job! I was never on time, and that got on their last nerve. I am a night owl, and it was a struggle to get there at 1:00 PM.

I wanted to get work on TV or in films, and I knew I had to get real and serious. I passed through acting technique sessions with Sanford Morris, Sam Groom, and Jeanne Kaplan. I took so many classes at HB that the school became my crib. I even took another comedy class at The Gotham Comedy Club with Dan Vitale. I probably enjoyed all those classes as much as any real gig in "the business."

Not long after, I was in a play called *Mishkin's Paradise*. We did it at The Producers' Club in New York City. It was a smash! The actors had a good time doing it, and I had fun. I am happy Fred included me as "Rose/Sadie" in the production.

Soon, I had a chance to have a major role in an independent film, but during my audition over dinner with the film writer, Robert Siegel, at The Chelsea Gallery Diner, I stopped and recommended another actor for the part. She was famous, and he hired her. Why did I do that? I have no answer except to say the concept of being in a film was starting to not have that much appeal and my obstacles sabotage my own life. In the end, I was a total flop at "getting real." The only thing is that the actor, who got that part because of me, lives in my neighborhood, and she sees me all the time, and she never even thanked me. That really bothered me.

So my dream was to become a movie star. That never happened. I was not a risk taker and stayed with that day job for almost thirty-five years. And after retirement, I got cold feet. I feel I spent much of my life hiding under the bed.

A few years later, I reinvented myself and created "Yetta Telebenda" and began daily live broadcasts on the internet. I became sort of cyber famous. The show is a partial verbal memoir, and I discuss my life and talk about some aspects of my personal history and experiences. I do comedy sketches, dramatic readings, sing, and do impressions. And years ago, I also did some live broadcasts on the streets of NYC. My life as Yetta has been filled with adventures. I have many fans, and I make them laugh.... and oh, I have trolls too. Success!

When a "fan" sent me this message, I was moved:

> *There is a man I read about who leaves fresh flowers for his deceased wife every single day. I want to do the same thing for you years down the line along with reading a newly written letter aloud to you every day and I will end it with "Goodnight Yetta, wherever you are."*

Everything happens for a reason. In many ways, I feel I disappointed my younger self, who had so many hopes and dreams. I am sorry, little Marjorie. But maybe in some small-scale way I actually did "make it." And life moves as quickly as hot butter on cold snow.

8 ~ *The Bumps in the Road: vignettes*

I Used to Live Here as a Kid

I TOOK THAT SPECIAL RIDE today, back to the street and house where I grew up. I parked my car and walked up the same driveway I had walked up thousands of times so many years ago when that house belonged to my family. I climbed the three front porch steps and peeked in through the glass front door, but the interior was barely visible: all dark and muted. It was a different house, not my house. I rang the bell, and nobody answered. I gathered nobody was home because the mailbox was stuffed and full.

So, I turned around and walked down the three front porch steps and then turned around and looked back. It was almost dusk and chilly under a cloudy, grey sky, and the wind rustled some long, tall plants in front of the living room's bay window. They swayed back and forth, back and forth. I was overwhelmed with a great and almost unbearable sadness.

Nobody was home, and nobody would ever be back home there for me. The street was bleak, depressing, and unrecognizable... the houses seemed forlorn and like shadows of their former selves. The streets where children once played and rode their bikes were empty. The stream where we once caught tadpoles and watched them change to frogs was dry. There was silence where once there was noise. Going back that day was personally like visiting a cemetery. There was so much emptiness, and a great feeling of loss. The wind kept rustling the front shrubbery, rustling the shrubbery, and as I stood all alone on that sidewalk, for a minute it felt like nobody even lived on that street. Everybody was gone. The street was a gloomy ghost town.

I thought of my bedroom in that house where I would look out of my window and see the lights from the back of the houses behind our house. I could still hear the neighbors talking from a time long gone, as they had dinner on their patio and played music from long ago.

I got back into my car and drove away, consumed with strange, heavy emotions. I will always think of that street. Always. I knew I would never go back there again... but as the view of that street disappeared in the rear view mirror, I remembered the time so many years ago when I drove away from that street into the city and moved into the apartment where I still live.

Part Two

Misery Had
No Company

Joe's Camp

WHAT CAN I SAY ABOUT "Joe's Camp?" It was an ad hoc camp for kids that gathered in my backyard. We fooled around and played silly games. I suppose only very immature nine-year-olds would get such a kick out of telling Joe, at snack time, to pour the Hawaiian Punch into our paper cups, which we pulled away before they were full.

We watched and laughed like drunken hyenas as the liquid spilled all over the patio, much to the delight of the ants who licked their chops over that daily sticky treat. And the dangerously broken swing set in that 1956 backyard added just the right touch of decadence.

Camp sure was "camp." This is a true bittersweet memory that, over time, has become my cult classic. It's my madeleine.

The First Experience at Sleep-Away Summer Camp

DURING THE SUMMER OF 1957, I spent two weeks at a camp on Long Island. It was almost the two most miserable weeks of my life, of which there were many. And I was more than homesick. I was so unhappy, I think I became catatonic.

What made it so terrible was that I was allowed to remain so upset and fall into a condition that is clearly visible in photos of the time I was there. The camp provided good meals. But I had lost my appetite. The first dinner there was Swedish meatballs, and I can still recall biting into one of those meatballs and pulling out a long piece of hair from my mouth.

Then, when we had a night picnic, some counselor loaded up my paper plate with fried chicken and corn, and the weight of it made it tilt, and the food tumbled to the ground. And after all who saw it laughed, nobody gave me a refill. It was a night of hunger.

Even camping out in a tent on the beach made me miserable. I was cold, and they threw some rubber blanket on me, perhaps in some obtuse way referencing me as a wet blanket. I felt trapped in a nightmare. I recall waking up early one morning and I was sharing my bed with a grasshopper. The girl next to me sat on her cot and laughed. The girls had short-sheeted my bed the night before, and I guess the grasshopper was the prank's dessert.

For some reason, all the other girls went to activities in the afternoons. They even went swimming. I had not signed up for anything, so I was left alone in the cabin to cry. I mean, sob. I wrote my mother a letter and ordered her to pick me up and get me the hell out of there. Then, a few hours after I put it in the mailbox, I trekked down the hill to retrieve it. I didn't want to upset my mother. But, when my parents visited, the sight of me upset them plenty. My parents visited me after the first week, and they were appalled at how I looked. I had lost a great deal of weight, and for some reason, my hair was so short. And I stank.

Somebody had neglected to show me where the showers were. I had not eaten, and my parents brought me chocolate milk that was so good that when I close my eyes today, I can still taste the gooey, rich sweetness. And they fed me the first meal I was able to eat in almost five days. I was never skinny in my whole life. The camp was able to bring on my skinny. And it was not a weight loss camp.

I think as I walk around today, the unhappiness of those two weeks still lives inside me within a small corner of my mind and brings me to dark places for which I can never quite pinpoint a reason. My parents had asked me if I wanted to go home with them. And why, when my parents visited after the first week of the two, did I not go home? I have no answer except to say I was not a quitter, so I stayed. I should have been diagnosed as a masochist and sent home in an ambulance.

Summer Memories with
Margaret Bourke-White

FOR THREE NIGHTS IN AUGUST 1961, I slept next to the world-famous photographer Margaret Bourke-White. I was right there, sleeping right next to her, in a small wooden cabin on Martha's Vineyard that actually could only fit two cots and a small dresser. She had the bed on the left side next to the trees, and I slept in the bed closer to the water on the other side. The space was sort of cluttered.

The cabin was in Vineyard Haven on the grounds of The School of Creative Arts, a summer camp owned and managed by Kathleen Hinni, who was the dance instructor at The Chapin School in New York City. Miss Bourke-White had Parkinson's Disease, and she chose to spend quiet summers at the camp on Martha's Vineyard with her friend, Miss Hinni. A few of her celebrated photos hung in the main house's living room.

I slept there because I was sick. The procedure was for campers who fell ill to pack up and go to stay with Miss Bourke-White, in that cabin's designated "sick bed." So, for three nights,

I lay there sick as a dog and rather unaware of her presence or the magnitude of the great accomplishments of the remarkable woman who slept next to me.

What I do remember is that in the middle of one of those nights, I was awakened by a head counselor who told me that one of the girls in my cabin had taken an excessive amount of pills. I knew this camper was very unhappy and had plans to "run away" from camp and spend a day in town with her boyfriend, who looked like Sal Mineo. SOCA was for girls only, and we were all terribly homesick, boy crazy, and hungry in so many ways.

All summer long, the campers danced, and on hot days, we gazed at the water and jumped in and out of cabins for fun. Days were simple and uncomplicated back then. I spent four summers at that camp. Even though our days were filled with inspiring and creative activity, I longed to be elsewhere.

I wanted to be at our beach club on Long Island, flirting with the cabana boy, and at the end of the day, I preferred to watch *American Bandstand* and read the comic strip *Brenda Starr*. And having the time to read a good Nancy Drew sounded marvelous. So if I was so unhappy, why did I keep going back? Did I have a choice? Still to this day, when I hear a ferry foghorn, I am reminded of those lonely times when that sound filled the air of Vineyard Haven and made so many of us yearn to be any place... but there.

My European Vacation

THIS WAS MY EXPERIENCE DECADES ago, during the summer of 1969. It is not a cautionary tale or foolish advice for others. I know many friends and relatives who constantly travel all over the world to the most remote and exotic places, and love it. But this particular piece tells of my time in Europe. And to this day, those two weeks are memorable. The depression and loneliness were unbearable.

So what could go wrong with a TWA Travel Adventure? My trip was ruined not because of the travel locations but because I had the misfortune of going with two "mean girls" who left me stranded and alone in every city we visited.

Barbara and I planned the trip to Lisbon, Madrid, Paris, and Rome. I did not realize that when Barbara invited Ilene (who would already be in Europe) to meet up with us at our first city location... my trip would immediately go south. Destination agony.

I was timid back then and very shy and quiet. I suppose

that demeanor made me a bully magnet: a target for the unresolved angers of others... in school, in camp, and in so many other places in my life. So when that "mean girl" Ilene talked dopey, weak-minded Barbara into flat-leaving me and going off on daily explorations without me, Barbara agreed, and off they went, abandoning me to be alone every day to decide whether, after leaving the hotel, I should wander left or go roam right. The only good day I had was going with my friend Tina to the Louvre, a meet-up we had planned before we even left Manhattan, since we knew we would be crossing paths during our two separate vacations. I had one night with the two sadistic mental torturers: I have a photo of the three of us in a Madrid cafe. Trust me, the misery on my face in the picture from that night is palpable.

Seriously, who does that? What kind of "friends" trot off and leave another girl behind to spend days and nights alone in foreign cities? I do not think it was a plan. I think Ilene instigated it, and the lemming Barbara followed along.

And if that was in Barbara's ability, why didn't she let me back out when I had a change of mind about even going? That fool called my mother to tell her she should convince me to still go. And of course, my mother put some guilt inside me, saying I would ruin Barbara's summer if I did not go.

My mother: always siding with anybody except her own daughter.

In Rome, those two horrible girls, Barbara and Ilene, talked me into going to an isolated beach house (at some deserted location) with three guys they had just met that day. That night, we arrived there after a 45-minute drive. It was very dark, and nobody else was even around. In that cabin, most of the light bulbs were broken, and there was no working toilet. Some bed was turned on the side, and all the furniture was broken. It was just a long, wide empty beach under a bright moon... and us: three guys and three girls. It was straight out of a horror movie. I think I passed out. I cannot remember how we got back to the hotel. Years later, I wondered if they used the interior of that place for the set of the film *Hostel*.

I remember being alone in the Lisbon hotel room one night (once again, Barbara and Ilene flat-left me, going off for perhaps another dangerous escapade) and wishing that when I opened my eyes, the two weeks for that trip would be over. I just wanted to go home. I was so tired of having every dinner alone in a foreign country, and I felt so deserted. I even got paranoid that my food was poisoned. I lost a great deal of weight during those two weeks away. I should market my life experiences as a quick weight loss program.

Anyway, even though we were an organized TWA group, we did not have structured days... we only gathered at the airports, and every experience at customs was a personal nightmare. Did I look suspicious? Did I look like a smuggler? My unlocked luggage was always picked for inspections. Always. Every. Single. Time. I had actual hallucinations that drugs would be planted in my suitcases, and I would be framed. I began to feel there was some nefarious plot to throw me into a prison, and that was decades before reality TV shows created episodes around that theme.

I believe the fear from that summer and that trip triggered my OCD. I was very young, changing, and at that time, I just did not have the skills or confidence to handle the matter or manage my situation. Of course, I probably had a tendency to develop an anxiety disorder because I was a nervous kid and a worrier, but that trip in 1969 sealed the deal. I spent years after that going into panics that never impacted others but certainly thwarted my own life. And after that traumatic and hurtful experience that summer, I got off easy. I could have developed agoraphobia.

And though I have since traveled many times to diverse locations, I never went back to Europe. Perhaps as I developed and grew older, I would have had a great time alone in those wonderful cities. After that year, I spent many summer days at Long Beach, Long Island. For decades, I never had to travel far to find a place that gave me strange peace.

Reflections on Misery
and Magical Thinking

IT FALLS AWAY AS VIVID and ongoing chapters of my childhood to accept that I was the go-to kid to be teased and picked on. Certainly, in elementary school, I was always the last to be picked for everything. I got it. I was a slow runner and lazy at every game. Lori chided me during kickball with "Exert yourself, Marjorie," and I thought, "I am." And whichever team got me, there was always a girl in the group to taunt me with: "Ew, you got Marjorie." I was the "Ew Girl."

I fell into that role of never being popular and always the loser... and my experience at Camp Baumann was no exception. Another experience of misery. I was literally sent off to a day camp every single day, which was torture. Nothing new there. I hated swimming, I hated sports, and I hated arts and crafts. The girls ostracized me. The boys abused me during every bus ride there and back by pulling on clumps of my hair. I am surprised that at the end of the summer, I still had hair on my head.

A kid on my block, Robin, once gathered her snark and

said about sleep-away summer camp: "There's a freak in every bunk." And I was always that freak. At The School of Creative Arts, the girls gave me the name "Bird Dog." I sort of got it. I was fat and ugly, with acne to boot. I always owned that role. And high school continued to define me within that part. I remember not wanting to even see my own reflection in a mirror because I thought I looked like what today would be called "cringe." This kid, Chris, would ridicule me right to my face and call me a "zero, beast." Back then, "shaming" was *de rigueur*. I was a real bully magnet and the poster child for unhappiness. There are a few specific times that live in my memory.

I remember when I was about nineteen, I had a double-blind date, and I was picked up first. When we arrived at the other girl's house, and I got out of the car to get the other girl, those two guys drove away, making a fast getaway. I concluded I was too ugly for even one night in the dark at a movie.

There was one specific time, probably the most hurtful, that sticks with me. It happened on New Year's Eve of 1963, going into 1964, at The Concord Hotel. I had planned my outfit well in advance. I wore a blue velvet and white satin dress with a green silk sash, and had my shoes dyed green to match the dress. My mother told me I would be sitting that night at a table with other teens, all of whom were total strangers to me. My sister sat at a pre-teen table and my parents sat at a table with other adults. So there I was, at a round table with three other girls and four boys. The girls were pretty and giving off a real Sandra Dee vibe. The boys looked like Frankie Avalon or maybe Fabian.

And I looked sort of like a fat, very ugly version of pretty Annette Funicello. For some reason, all of those teens at my table decided to abandon our table number 10 and join table 11, which had some empty seats. So all seven of them filled those empty seats and left me sitting all alone. I thought I should at least try to sit with them, so I got up and boldly asked if they could fit me and my chair in. One of those boys brazenly said, "There is no room," and the girls laughed.

I sat back alone at my table, and I cried. I was so overwhelmed with sadness. I was so hurt. I was not going to sit there and eat alone. My face must have been soaking wet because when I left that table, and I went to the other side of that dining room to tell my mother I was going back up to the room, she did ask what happened. But I quickly fled out of that ballroom and went upstairs. When I was back in the room, I put on the TV and watched the old film *Not As A Stranger*. Every time I see that movie on TCM, I remember that night.

Oh, I saw one of my high school bullies, Chris, at a 30-year high school reunion and asked him why he tormented me so much back then, and without missing a beat, he called himself an "asshole." I liked that answer.

And oh, those teens from that night at The Concord Hotel so long ago? Who knows where they are now? They are probably all dead.

And even when I was in college, I went to get a haircut at a local salon, and one of the stylists who was not working at the time left to get a sandwich. When she returned, she was not alone. She actually went in to the hardware store in that little strip mall and returned with some guy who entered and declared sarcastically, "I hear you have a real winner in here." And they all laughed.

Was I, during childhood and throughout college, a bully magnet? Obviously, yes. Even my own mother made fun of me in multiple ways all the time. For instance, being called a "bump on a log" and being told I had "no personality" certainly were a few of the insults that did not come from the mouths of my peers. I tell my viewers in my internet broadcast that I am immune to harassment because my own mother trolled me during my entire childhood. She exacerbated every hurtful situation in layered ways, and in retrospect, she was my Bully Number Zero.

My mother never helped with my appearance, and she certainly never raised my level of confidence. The only time she inserted herself into my clothing choices (and the selection was very limited) was when I told her I was going into Manhattan, and she told me I had to wear silk stockings because I was going into "the city." She respected "the city" more than she ever did me.

She had a huge negative impact on my development, and when I was a teenager, her damage was severe. She never missed a day of hurling insults at me, and she knew I had a few teen crushes, and her response was always put-downs, making comments such as "Why would he be interested in you?" Or "Shut up about him already." I could list so many more ways she validated her mental illness, but why allow her to hijack these vignettes?

But here is one doozy: My friend Sharon told me that Betty's mother took out her eyeballs every night and washed them. That story should have been categorized as a Valley Stream "Urban Legend." But when I told my mother about that, without missing a beat, she replied: "Betty's mother has the right idea." The woman needed heavy doses of Haldol.

There was not one time "that woman" showed any concern for my happiness or well-being. Maybe those early experiences drove my nature to make anxiety my default setting within a weird comfort zone. As somebody close to me once said, "It is a miracle you did not turn to drugs or alcohol to handle all of that." And I didn't.

A few short years after I moved away, I was determined to create a new visual version of myself. There was no way I was going to age and grow old into that defined nightmare. I firmly believed that I could change my appearance and change my life. I believed in strong ways. I was committed to shedding that image like a reptile. So I manifested my own version of *The Enchanted Cottage*.

And lo and behold, one day I awakened and looked in the mirror and I resembled Elizabeth Taylor! Fact. Not long after, I was stopped on East 57th Street and asked if I was Sophia Loren! When I was in Bonwit Teller, a woman said she was a painter and told me I was gorgeous! Was I dead and dreaming? And I remember the day when a custodian visited a school in which I was teaching, and he told me, "I have never seen a teacher so beautiful." Somehow, in an almost surreal way, I woke up at the age of twenty-three and had a different face! I also had a high level of confidence and excellent self-esteem. It had to be magical thinking! You can't make this stuff up!

I am reminded of the time when I was in first grade, and the class was in the schoolyard at recess. I was wearing a fine yellow dress with fancy red flowers, and I climbed the steps of the slide. I sat at the top and prepared to go down. As I took that first push, both sides of my dress caught on hooks on the top step of the slide. I shot down, and my dress pulled back over my body and arms and over my head and then tore off me, and I went down almost butt naked. When I reached the bottom, all I had on were my panties, and all the kids were pointing and laughing.

I ran at breakneck speed through the playground into the school as my dress flapped high above me in the wind. I landed straight in the nurse's office, and she gave me another dress to wear for the day. When I got home, my mother saw I was wearing a different dress and asked, "What happened?" I replied: "I fell backwards off my chair, hit my head, and threw up on my dress." Why exacerbate the embarrassment further?

Part Three

The Face That Could Have Launched 1,000 Hips

Fantasies, Lies, and Decades Later… the Internet

I HAVE GREETING CARDS WHICH are pieces of a bittersweet memory from 1971 to 1973, and the messages are quite romantic. I saved the cards to always remember a man I loved named Lou. But this was a dark and layered and mysterious "love" because Lou was not just a man... he was my therapist. Lou looked like Al Pacino in *Serpico*. And he was married with several children. So here goes.

I began seeing a therapist in about 1970. His office was in Greenwich Village, and after just a few sessions, I fell under the seductive spell of "erotic transference." I grew attached, and I was dependent. I was in love, or thought I was in love. The feelings were not yet mutual. There arrived the day when Lou told me he was moving his practice to Staten Island. I was not ready at all for the separation, and I was emotionally devastated. So, I followed him to Staten Island and became a weekly ferry regular.

The longing for him until my session each week was unbearable. I was vaguely aware back then that transference was a common feeling when in analysis. And I had fallen deeply in love with my therapist. Lou sent a real mixed bag of messages: he allowed me to believe the feelings were mutual, and at the end of each session, he drove me back to the ferry. His behavior was mercurial: by turns encouraging me with contact that crossed a line, and then emotionally pushing me away, and then he pulled me back in for more games.

He played with my desire. He sent me greeting cards for Valentine's Day and my birthday. He promised to meet me for lunch in Manhattan, and then he told me to find another therapist. I returned home filled with longing, and I was confused and desperately unhappy. I was in anguish. I wrote him long love letters filled with desperation. I was losing my mind.

The heartbreaking, bizarre saga continued for several years, and well… as it goes with time, the hypnotic spell eventually broke, and I ended the "therapy." One day, just like that.

About eight years later, in 1981, I called Lou's old number. I needed closure. Lou was very excited and happy to hear from me. He was divorced. He started manically calling me twice a day. I had to tell him to calm down. Soon, we had dinner at a Manhattan restaurant. He sat there all pompous and clueless, smoking a cigar. He made me sick. I had perspective and was more angry with myself and my own stupidity than with him. Nevertheless, we went back to my apartment, and when he left, I knew I would never see him again. He had not changed. He had told me over dinner that his experience with me took him to a place where he made a decision to never allow physical contact with a patient in a session ever again. The man was a fast and quick study!

I look back on this episode of my life now, and it is totally meaningless. I am not angry. I feel nothing. I know this goes on. Lou was verbally unprofessional, unethical, and his behavior was inconsistent. He did not know what to do about me, and he could not handle or come to terms with his own feelings. Transference is serious and should be handled properly by those who have fallen under its seductive spell. I think my experience with Lou exacerbated my condition of limerence, and I actually never knew I had that until a viewer in my broadcast was listening to one of my many stories and gave it a name. I am happy I saved all of Lou's cards because I am reminded of a bittersweet chapter of my life.

A few years ago, I saw on the internet that Lou had passed away. I called a number I believed could have been his (to offer some form of condolences to whoever answered). A woman picked up, and she told me she was his wife, allowing me to conclude he remarried. After some quick back story to identify myself, I asked her if Lou ever mentioned me. She said no... and as my saga unfolded, she was riveted by my story and listened intently. She actually seemed to enjoy hearing it. Damn, why am I so sad that he is gone? Maybe because I really would have liked to talk to him again.

As I advanced through the decades, did I experience great romance? The love of my life, after the Lou insanity, melted away into what was only a fantasy of what I believed him to be. As I grew older, I grew into enjoying solitude. I did not enjoy attachment, and some are just meant to "do alone." I was not to age as a "we," and any significant other felt like I was passing through time pulling a suitcase on wheels. Sad? Maybe.

Al Goldstein and Me

IN THE EARLY 1990s, I would go to a New York City restaurant (long closed) called Mulholland Drive Cafe on Sundays with Angie, another teacher. It was on Third Avenue around 64th Street, and it was owned by a well-known actor. The place was not that big, and it was a weekly hangout for Al Goldstein and his hangers-on... and plenty of adult film stars surrounded him. It was "Al this and Al that," and even though it was 1:00 PM, they dressed with a lot of sparkle and glitter like they were going to a disco. Plus, I never saw heels so high.

He was the center of attention, and he sat on his throne there at some long table at literally a higher level on a balcony at the top of a few steps. Al Goldstein, creator of the very popular sex magazine *Screw* and the host of *Midnight Blue* on public access TV, was sort of famous back then in New York City. He was considered a great pioneer within the world of porn.

After a few weeks, Al became more interested in me and Angie than his regular crew. So he sat with us, and after we gave him some back story and information about us, he said one of his ex-wives was a teacher. So then the conversation became all about the schools, a subject that always got me talking. It still does.

    Years after that, Al was living near me... on 8th Avenue and 15th Street, and if he passed my building when I was outside, we would stand on the sidewalk and talk for a while, always about the schools. He seemed lonely, and he would talk about his son. He was so proud of him.

    In 2004, he started working at the old Second Avenue Deli. He was almost broke and unrecognizable. Al passed away in 2013.

    Later, in about 2014, I was sitting with Robin Byrd at a comedy club holiday party. We talked about the old Channel J, and even about Steve Gruberg, whom I also knew from the neighborhood and whose cable TV show I would call from time to time. Steve also passed away.

Part Four

A Stream
of Consciousness

Memories of the Stylers

IT WAS IN 1968 THAT I first met the lovely and kind Mrs. Frances Styler. We were both teachers at PS 41, on West 11th Street in New York City's Greenwich Village. I was in my first year of teaching, and I was assigned a K-1 class. Mrs. Styler was there to help. We became fast friends, and she seemed to want to cultivate an out-of-school friendship with me. Mrs. Styler was married to a highly respected physician, and they lived in a brownstone on a leafy, quiet street not far from the school. Mrs. Styler invited me to lunch at her home on a school holiday, and I accepted. This experience is another that sticks with me, and today... on this unusually warm winter Saturday, memories are flooding back to me.

I remember it was on a Tuesday afternoon when I walked down from Chelsea to visit the Stylers for lunch. I rang the bell, and the door was answered by a member of her staff. I had never been to a home with a butler before, but he took my coat and showed me to the parlor, where I waited for Mrs. Styler. She entered, wearing exquisite formal attire. She greeted me, and then Dr. Styler entered to be introduced. He shook my hand and apologized that he would not be joining us for lunch because he had an emergency with a patient.

Mrs. Styler asked me if I needed to use the washroom, and she told me it was on the third floor to the left. I climbed the two long, steep flights of stairs and entered an elegant bathroom that appeared to be her personal boudoir. There was a chaise lounge and dressing tables filled with creams, perfumes, and dusting powders. Feathered robes and dressing gowns hung on the back of the door. And next to the sink were pink guest soaps in the shape of seashells.

I descended those long stairs and was escorted to the dining room table that could easily have seated twenty people. Mrs. Styler rang a bell, and her cook (in retrospect, she was straight out of *Downton Abbey*) entered to serve the appetizer. We dined on some fancy, prepared gourmet meal, and I had "paté." Mrs. Styler was very attentive to my level of comfort, and every time I made a request, she would ring the little soft bell, and her cook would appear and handle all the needs.

We discussed teaching and life. Mrs. Styler spoke about her daughter, who was about my age and whom she adored. We talked about many things. It was the first time I had been surrounded by such elegance.

It has been over fifty years since that day. I Googled around trying to find out where some of the many people I've crossed paths with during my long career are today. In my search, I sadly learned Mrs. Styler passed away in 1999, and her husband passed away in 2004.

Manhattan was a quieter city forty years ago. There was a less rushed and congested atmosphere. People were less angry and not as confrontational. There was less noise. People seemed to treat each other more kindly. And everybody took time... to just breathe.

Michael Gazzo Asks Permission

THE YEAR WAS 1974. I was teaching at a small school on West 45th Street. I had a wonderful sixth-grade class. The students were bright, creative, and they had a real sense of humor. The school was not far from the Actor's Studio; the Manhattan Plaza had just been completed, and on nice days I could walk home. I loved going to work.

One day, a student named Chris came to school a little bit late. I asked him the reason for his tardiness, and he told me that the night before, he had attended an opening of a movie in which his father had a role. I asked him the name of the film, and he replied, *The Godfather Part II*.

"Oh," I said. I asked, "What part did your father have in the movie?"

He replied, "Frankie Pentangeli."

I knew that Chris's father was the well-known playwright, Michael Gazzo, but I did not know that he was in the film, *The Godfather Part II*. So! Chris's father was Frankie Pentangeli, interesting...

The Godfather Part II was released, and it opened at a Loew's theater on Broadway. It received phenomenal reviews, and I couldn't wait to see it. Mr. Gazzo had written a note to me during that school year asking permission for his son to be excused early on an October day, and I saved the note. It was not just a signed note; it was an autograph.

A few months later, the Gazzo family moved to Los Angeles. Chris kept in touch with all of us through letters he sent to the school, addressed to me. In one letter, Chris asked me if I was still singing because I was awful. I was a teacher who sang while she taught? (My "bad singing" has developed into my personal brand of performance art on my current internet broadcast). Chris said he was going to a school twenty times better, but he would rather be going to our school because he missed all of us.

I think about all of the students I had in so many classes over the years. I loved being a teacher: Every day, I had a place to go.

Intermission: Lighten Up!

My stand-up comedy was so bad I was rejected from *The Gong Show*.

I wrote a book and in a week it was on the dollar table at The Strand.

I sucked on a salt stick, and my blood pressure soared, and that triggered my OCD and I started cleaning the fire escape.

I am so germ phobic I put on plastic gloves to use my own toothbrush.

I took Home Economics in high school, and I got an A in Elements of a Successful Marriage and I am still single!

I had two students who were real inventive. Every sunny day they took seats near the window and used magnifying glasses to see who could burn the fastest hole into my left eyeball.

In high school, I failed a history final exam with a 63 and I went to summer school and got a 41. Who could learn in such heat?

A student signed his homework with the name *The Seed of Chucky* and another used the name *Rosemary's Baby*. I wrote on the chalkboard: My name is *Carrie*.

Part Five

My Mosh Pit

Three Love Letters

I FOUND TWO OLD, LONG-FORGOTTEN photos while rummaging through an old shoebox. I also found three letters from a summer of long ago:

August 3rd
Dear J:
    I want to tell you what happened on a hazy, hot, sunless Sunday, in July, at Long Beach. A few feet from where an amnesiac sat on the boardwalk eating hotdogs—a lady, a blue blood, and a wanderer observed in the sand a mystical image. Well, because they were frightened that the startling sight might rapidly disappear or be scrambled by an insouciant breeze, an attempt was made by the lady to photograph the sight—to freeze and thereby validate the remarkable event. The lady put down her translucent parasol and a love letter that was written in Sanskrit on an ancient, faded doily. And as a tow-headed child paddled to shore in a teacup, a picture was taken and developed. It passed

from the lady to the blue blood, and then to the wanderer— from whose tired, careless fingers it slipped. The wind carried the picture down and up, up and down; it danced the tango for a few seconds before it collapsed in my open right hand. I swear, J, in that photograph I saw the transmigration of a soul!
Kindest regards,
M

August 12th
Dear M:
    I love you and want to marry you! Why didn't you tell me you were spending July out at Long Beach? I desperately wanted you to know that I enrolled in a film workshop, and I will complete the requirements and be eligible for a certificate in film. By the way, the theme of my first project is reincarnation. I wish you were with me, supporting my cinematic aspirations and visions. Last Tuesday, while I dined at an outdoor sidewalk cafe on Columbus Avenue, a lady passed holding a translucent parasol. She was walking her Shih Tzu, and when she paused in front of my table, she allowed her thirsty pet to take a few swigs from a bottle of seltzer. I took a picture of the lady and her dog, and I am sending it to you.
Love,
J

August 28th
Dear J:
    Your letter was forwarded to me from the Long Beach address. I am now staying in Westhampton. While I was having

dinner at a restaurant in East Hampton, I was introduced by a man called Kevin to a group of young Buddhists. In the early mornings, I joined them at a mansion for the recitation of five prayers. I want to tell you what happened at the beach on a hot, sunny Sunday in mid-August. A dilettante, a pacifist, and a codependent led me to a spiritual man, who for a short time in July posed as an amnesiac at Long Beach. He now conducts a series of past life regression sessions, and I was persuaded to participate. As I reclined on the Westhampton sand, a lonely seagull flew overhead, and a tow-headed child paddled, in a teacup, to shore. In time, I recalled a past life! I realize now, Jason, that we were together as lovers during the French Revolution.

So, I will be returning to Manhattan at the end of August, and we shall plan our wedding.

Love, xxxooo,

M

The Milgram Experiment and Me

I WAS PART OF THE Milgram Experiments in the mid-1960s while I was attending C.W. Post College on Long Island. I was recruited for this role in my psychology class. I was Person A and seated in a small room with some electronic devices. I was "the teacher," and I was instructed to ask questions to Person B, who was "the student" and who was in another room. If my student answered incorrectly, I was told to administer shocks. The levels and strength of the shocks were my decisions. Oh, by the way, in order to gauge how that shock machine worked, at the beginning I was given the lowest shock. How rude! And there was a person (experimenter) in another room reminding and encouraging me to give high-strength shocks for wrong answers.

    I will be very honest. I realized when I was introduced to Person B before the experiment began that she was not really going to be shocked. (Yes, we saw our "victims/students" before the questions and "shocks"). And during the experiment, the person giving the instructions was weak-sounding. I was not surprised at the end of the experiment when my "student/victim" and the "experimenter/voice" came out of the other room laughing. I thought the whole thing was a transparent farce. I wonder how many other participants realized it was phony. I figured it out right away.

The participants were both lousy actors. Despite the transparency, I gave minimal shocks, and I did not become a torturer, perhaps foiling their predictions. It was just so not my thing.

Me and My Baby Teeth

DENTISTS ARE ALWAYS SURPRISED WHEN they examine my teeth and find I still have three baby teeth. They just never fell out. There may be no permanent teeth under them, which might be the reason they are still in my mouth. I love them. I have had them for over seventy years. I fear I may have a huge cavity in one of my baby teeth because it has been sensitive, and it hurts. It was explained to me that the tooth cannot be refilled with amalgam because very little of the tooth structure remains. They cannot do a root canal on a baby tooth, and it cannot be capped. It might have to be extracted. My fear is exacerbated.

I am very puerile and immature. I have the *joie de vivre* of a much younger woman. Plus, I sort of do not look my age. Are you with me here? Are you following this? You got it.

I fear that when I lose my baby teeth, I will rapidly age. A few short days after my baby teeth are extracted, I will look all wrinkled, bent, and wizened. And my youthful sense of self-deprecating humor will disappear.

I allude to a biblical story. Samson's hair is what made him so strong. Delilah found out it was because his hair had never been cut. When his hair was cut, he lost his strength. Also think: *The Picture of Dorian Gray*, but not quite… Yes, my baby teeth are my Fountain of Youth. They keep me young. They may in fact, contain Botox. They may drip collagen into my system. Maybe they even produce a quickly absorbed form of Retinol. But what concerns me most about the loss of my remaining baby teeth is that I will morph into a boring, droll, and trite crone. No longer will my internet fans be sweatin' Da BAD SiNGin' EDuCaTor, they will be watching Miss Old Biddy.

A Ghost Story

I WAS DOWN IN THE basement doing laundry. As I was loading a washing machine, a young, friendly woman named Darlene (who lives on the second floor) came down. As she moved her clothes into a dryer, she hummed a soft tune. She told me she just moved in, and we started talking. I have lived here for decades, and she asked me about the building. I told her many stories, and she seemed fascinated by the history of the place. I said that some residents believe the building is haunted. She laughed and groaned, "Shuttt uppppppp."

I told her that in 1969, a man who lived next door to me committed suicide. He played creepy music every night, and on a stormy night, I heard screams mixed with strong howling winds. The next day, his body was found in the back of the building in a pile of wet snow. He had jumped out of the window.

Since then, many residents who have lived in that apartment say they sometimes see a man covered in snow behind their shoulder when they are looking into the bathroom mirror.

In the 1970s, on Sunday mornings, a group of fun guys used to dance in the back courtyard to the soundtracks of different Broadway shows. Sometimes they presented entire scenes while dressed in elaborate costumes. *West Side Story* was their favorite. Every so often, we hear theater music back there, and nobody knows from where that music is coming.

Darlene and I continued to have a conversation, and soon it was time for her to go back upstairs. I asked her to wait a minute before she left, and then my expression became serene, and my eyes must have appeared unfocused and glazed. Darlene stared at me. I told her that tomorrow, when she tells people that the night before she spoke in the laundry room to a woman named Marjorie who lives in apartment 8S... they are going to tell her that Marjorie died ten years ago. She screamed, and goosebumps appeared on her skin. She backed away and declared, "Now THAT is not funny!" I never saw her again.

Part Six

Aliases For Potential Crybabies

MarjTheBombshell and Solly Boy, the Enforcer

I AM THE MARJTHEBOMBSHELL IN the title of this piece. Solly Boy is the other part of the two-person dynamic in the saga.

So back in 1999, when AOL was in its infancy, there were popular chat rooms where you could spend time and have fun talking to strangers, and maybe even meet those with whom you communicated. We had "screen names" that we used so our identity remained anonymous. I created "MarjTheBombshell," as a tribute to how I wanted to be perceived. It was a bit self-involved, but I got attention.

I never actually wanted to meet a man in a chat room and seriously "partner up." I did not think I was nothing without a man, and "getting married" was not in my wheelhouse as a reach for entelechy. I grew to actually like not being attached and enjoyed solitude and being alone after a hard day at work teaching sixth graders. But... I did like to socialize at that time, so when my "Singles Over 40" group started to plan local gatherings,

I was in. I loved meeting the faces behind the names. I loved hanging out on Friday nights at Long Island clubs and meeting this same group for occasional lunches in Queens restaurants. I lived in Manhattan (and still live here), and I had a car (I still have a car), and keep it in the garage under my building.

When one lunch was being planned, Paul, "NightCop," or something, I cannot remember, contacted me. I knew Paul from months of talking in that room, and in a bizarre coincidence, Paul was a business associate of my father. My father owned Columbia Silver Company, and Paul produced some items my father needed for an association. Paul asked me if I would take his friend to the restaurant on Woodhaven Boulevard, which was a short drive out of the Midtown Tunnel. He also told me his "friend" lived close by, on West 20th Street, and would meet me in the lobby of my building. "So what's his name?" I asked. "Solly Boy," Paul replied. He added he is known as "The Enforcer." I had read about him in the newspapers. He did hard time. His name speaks for itself. He was well known for his crimes, and at one time, he was featured on many tabloid-style TV shows.

"Will this be a problem?" Paul asked. He assured me it was safe. I was fine with it. What could happen? It was extreme to think he would whip out a gun and blow my head off.

This now comes flooding back: I was best friends in summer camp with a girl from Merrick who, years later, robbed houses at gunpoint, and it was in the newspaper. When I saw the article about her crimes in *Newsday*, I showed it to my mother, who replied without missing a beat, "It figures you'd be friends with her." At the time, I was not shocked by my mother's reaction because she was the queen of insults. She had three great enemies in life: her husband and her two daughters.

So the day came and there he was... in my lobby, ready for the day's adventure. We made small talk on the way out, the lunch was uneventful, and Solly flirted with Suzy. But the ride back to Manhattan was a different experience. We hit bad traffic, and Solly wanted to get back to attend a lecture at a university. His impatience was palpable, and he was growing angry. I was getting edgy. But we got back, and a block after we hit West 30th Street, Solly thanked me for the ride and jumped out of the vehicle.

Bye Solly. We never spoke again after that day. But I hear he likes taking long walks and feeding pigeons in the park.

Dumped by Benjamin Weiner

I FIRST SAW BENNY WEINER on October 24, 2008, at a Soap Opera Festival held in Newark, New Jersey. He moderated a very interesting panel discussion with some old soap stars. Benny also presented a loving tribute to his father, Manny, who was in the serial *The Secret Wedding* during the 1970s. He was known in comedy clubs as Manny the Heckler because he made fun of those in the audience. He passed away in March 2006.

I was very impressed with Benny's participation, so I went to the Drama Book Shop and bought his book, *The Son of a Heckler*, to learn more about him and his career. It turns out his grandfather is the famous comic Tiny Weiner. (Benny goes by his grandfather's surname). Benny's mother is the daughter of the infamous Tiny Weiner, who was a pioneer during television's golden age. Soon after that festival, I sent Benny an email.

Benny:
    I am almost finished reading *The Son of a Heckler*, and I

am loving it so much I am not wanting it to end. This is a fascinating story of a true journey... and I think what is so amazing is how the narrative is factually presented with visual memorabilia in photos and is also written with layers of extremely dark wit and humor. It is hilarious! I am just astounded by so many parts. And it is so well presented that I feel as if I am actually watching the sagas unfold. I think you did a great job showing in subtle ways how people interacted and related to your father. Benny, your book is just wonderful. Let me put it this way: it's a book that is the best independent film I have ever read.
Marjorie

Shortly after I sent the above email to Benny, I wrote to him again and asked if he would meet me for lunch. I have no boundaries. He immediately replied, "Sure," and we met on a Wednesday at noon at a diner on Upper Broadway in New York City. We started to talk, and right away I was impressed with Benny's straightforward, honest, and down-to-earth manner. He spoke about his musical, *Early to Bed*, and he said he regretted that the show's "time (on Broadway) was short." He discussed, in a very forthright manner, how the last few days of the show turned into a fiasco because the performers were not getting the response they expected. He wrote *Early to Bed* based on his relationship with his father at the time. His father never saw the show. Benny says in his book that his father blocked all communication with him because Benny did not go to Manny's last stand-up comedy show in upstate New York. The loss of the relationship was a huge disappointment to him that he lives with to this day.

I went to a few of Benny's book signings to show support for his endeavors and always had a good time. Benny has an extensive list of accomplishments. He had a salute to Brucie Decker, which he performed at a New York City nightclub, and he has done a few comedy albums. Benny was working on a musical about his father and included some of Manny's best lines:

"You are all better than a sleeping pill."

"If I could get this audience to laugh, I would make this night a tax deduction for my charity work."

"My last girlfriend watched me like a hawk, and she was up my ass more than a rectal suppository."

Benny Weiner, son of Manny the Heckler, stopped talking to me because I stopped going to his shows at New York City nightclubs. I did not go to his show where he sang the songs of Brucie Decker because I thought it would be torture. Benny was not a great singer, and to listen to him drone on for two hours while strumming his guitar would have been unbearable. Anyway, I think his shows were "bringers" where he was required to have a certain number of asses in seats, or he would not get stage time.

The last time I was asked to go to his show, I told him I had nobody to go with, and he said I could sit with his mother and his father's old comedy partner from the 1960s. But I had seen his show many times. How many book signings and shows did he want me to go to? He was also angry that I was not buying enough of his merch and stuff even though I bought two of his books and even his mother's book. So he cut me off...

Yikes. So immature. Didn't his father do that to him for the same reason?

Catfished

JEEVES, PASS THE SMELLING SALTS. In my broadcast now, I try to gain new insights into a specific emotional saga and to achieve a greater perspective and understanding of my choices during an earlier time when I was "catfished." And I was... for a long time.

I try to work through the confusion and to determine the motivations behind the behavior of the "other person" within the maze of numerous interactions that happened over the many years of a very bizarre period of my life. During the journey, I remained quiet and allowed it all to unfold in great mysteries "behind the scenes." It was layered, complicated, and filled with great contradictions. This was my lucid "trip" into the surreal world of the dark web, where bends in a personal dynamic confuse reality.

I did not love this stranger whom I met in my show back in 2013. We can call him "DarkCode." He watched my show and became obsessed with me. He never missed a show. We interacted in my chat room during my broadcast: with me "on cam," and he typed in the chat box and sent me private messages all day at a social media site. He never revealed his face and kept his true identity private, but he did send several photos, which he claimed were of him but were obviously not. He clearly was not who he said he was. But back then, he "got inside my head" with his manipulations and mind tricks. I became dependent on him as he advanced to becoming my videographer. He would record my shows as I broadcast from several New York City street locations.

Even though his identity was murky, he was eventually able to convince me that his emotional well-being and happiness were totally dependent on having me in his life on a computer. If I told him to "go away," he made me believe he was becoming very self-destructive. And he was jealous, controlling, and he created elaborate sagas in messages about adventures that were, by turns, entertaining and then alarming. He spent years creating detailed stories about his life, and I went down that rabbit hole as if I was hypnotized and in some trance.

This was a deep dive into mind bends and will be incomprehensible to many of those who live in the real world with grounded lives. To them, this will be totally impossible to even understand. They function in a tangible world with regular activity of traveling with a spouse, entertaining family, meeting friends for lunch, shopping, renovating, weekend getaways to country homes, and visits with the grandchildren. In other words, they thrive in and enjoy a senior reality.

That world: a world that alluded me. But, there is a subterranean subculture of bizarre "night owls" who interconnect with each other on social media and who allow feelings for others in that world to marinate internally. They move within a different world, a world of fantasy and even delusion. And those "kooks" will "get it." In my specific situation, I was enabling this catfish's "idea" of me... in all his full-blown delusional glory.

He even pulled others into his agenda... a woman named "Jinx" who contacted me and told me I was "walking him to his grave." She posted this to him, which I was able to see: "I will not stand over your grave! But I will go with you to it! And as long as I have a breath, she (me) will not be the reason!" They created a tag team for the purpose of manipulation to attach me to him for their own devious purposes.

Why did I allow this? I think the easiest reply is that I got caught up in a daily drama in which I was the main player and living within my own reality TV show. I could have blocked him, but that would have ended my own personal version of *The Truman Show*. He was insidious in multiple ways, and when you are being "gaslighted" by an expert, you make excuses for the emotional abuse and think you are ahead of it when, in fact, you are controlled and just a personal marionette for a catfish whose own needs are being fulfilled along the way.

Regardless of the level of fame, these characters crawl out of the woodwork and advance into the lives of the vulnerable within a twisted fantasy world. I had read about *The Miranda Obsession*, and it was said she was the first "catfish" during the 1970s and 1980s. She seduced, over the phone, many well-known high-profile men connected to Hollywood, and as those calls advanced, she sent fake photos. She was not who she said she was, and she may have met only one of them, and they continued to communicate with her for years.

Yes, cyber night crawlers do live in an alternate universe... a world of total limerence. But now, from where I sit, in some ways I feel I belong with them.

I slide into those esoteric relationships like a second skin.

Part Seven

Always Leave Them Wanting More

Bessie and the Expensive Coffin Theory

MY GRANDMOTHER LOVED TO BITCH about the relatives in Red Bank. She complained about everybody and everything, and she told us when she "dropped dead" not to bury her in "no expensive coffin." She said: "They are crooks. You buy a fancy coffin, and when you are at the cemetery, they lower you into it in the grave for show. Then everybody walks away, and when nobody is watching, later they take you out and plop you into the ground in nothing and cover you up with the dirt and resell that coffin. It's a big racket."

She died in 1967. I remember a day before she was buried, we went to see her at I.C. Plopper Funeral Home. She lay dead in a beautiful coffin, and I stared at her dead body in there. I could hear her calling to me from the beyond: "Marjala Mamala get me out of this here thing. I don't want no fancy coffin and be dumped later in the dirt."

I must have been standing there for some time because my mother came over and I said, "Remember what Grandma said about how she wanted to be buried in a cheap wood box?"

My mother looked surprised and said, "Yeah, she did say that. I remember her saying that when she sat on the piano bench." Then she told me to "Shut up and go sit down."

I was thinking about that today, and I think Grandma Bessie could have been onto something. I miss her. She was a wise woman.

I was also thinking about the time Bessie told me about this talking dog she saw on TV. On command, the dog would say "Mama."

My Mother Makes Joan Crawford Look Like Carol Brady

When I was sick, her response was: "What do you want me to do? I am not a doctor."

I recall when I woke up with a severe sore throat and told my mother, she said, "Brush your teeth." Remarkable. Maybe she thought she was into some cutting-edge holistic cure.

When we argued, her usual response was to tell me that "my true colors came out," which actually was letting me know she had some bizarre personality profile of me that was not flattering. It becomes interesting to note that she told that to me when I was twelve.

When any emotion was displayed by her children, her reaction was to check into the hospital with "a high blood pressure attack."

When I complained that I had too much work in college, she flew into a rage and ripped up my textbooks and my notebook with all of my Spanish literature translations.

Another gem she said, since I was thirteen: "You are waiting for me to die to get my money." And she died almost broke.

I could go on and list 100 other serious ways she validated she was severely abusive and psychotic, but why allow these vignettes to become my personal version of *Flowers in the Attic*?

Philosophy from The Crib

I THINK I GOT IT! The clue is in the "tachyons!" I believe in reincarnation, and superstring theory in quantum physics hints that it is possible to "time travel." When we "shuffle off this mortal coil," the consciousness is no longer confined by matter or gravity. The "tachyons" of the mind tunnel FTL through wormholes, at black holes, to one of an infinite set of parallel universes where we can be born again forward or backward in time.

Such beauty exists in this simplicity. It is our consciousness after death that is the ultimate time traveler. We are all time travelers!

Oh, what a journey! I am left breathless by the infinite possibilities! Maybe I will live on a street in Wilmette, which is my personal Willoughby. Perhaps one glorious day, I will sit with Jack Kerouac at The White Horse Tavern. Maybe I will be one of the dames hanging with The Rat Pack at The Sands Hotel. Maybe one great night, I will party with Marion Davies and William Hearst at San Simeon. I hope in a next life I remember not to book passage on the Titanic.

Can we begin to understand the strange cosmos? Perhaps physicists are not hard-wired to ever find the mysterious and elusive missing piece of the puzzle. Maybe we are just like little goldfish... goldfish that will never ever even understand that 1 + 1 = 2.

We all have a death sentence. But wait! We can get little stays of execution along the way. It's all about the postponements... the added time that allow us to continue enjoying whatever this is.

A Sunken Corridor

IN STARK CONTRAST TO NEW York City's Highline is the "sunken corridor," which is an area of old tracks between 10th and 11th Avenues, and they are visible on 45th Street through the cracks of the silver fences.

Many years ago, I took photos of that amazing sight and I was even able to take a picture of a train down below as it whizzed by. But all of the photos I took are lost. I now know that no trains even use those railroad tracks any longer. My great shots of that "phantom train" will exist only in my recollection as it rode quickly by on that rainy Thursday afternoon, carrying invisible passengers to some unknown downtown destination. That simple sight still sits on a vista in my mind where memories may one day move and vanish as quickly as that train on that misty day.

Thanks

To Cheryl Benton for her continued support.

And to the "Yetta Telebenda" fans who enjoyed my internet broadcasts and made me feel that I finally "made it."

About the Author

Marjorie J. Levine is a retired elementary school teacher. She is the author of *Road Trips, Becoming Until,* and *Moving Images*. She lives alone in NYC.

www.ingramcontent.com/pod-product-compliance
Lightning Source LLC
Chambersburg PA
CBHW020513030426
42337CB00011B/371